2

OBSERVATIONS
of an architect

Introduction

For as long as I can remember, I have had a heightened awareness of my surroundings. I sensed that I saw things a bit differently from other people, and often wondered why. I started writing about special moments that have stayed with me throughout my life to better understand their influence. Along with this writing, I was surveying the many thousands of photos I have taken from different times and locations, again, in an effort to distill what they mean to me. Both of these endeavors revealed several themes that form the basis of my approach to architecture.

As a collection of personal essays and images spanning more than twenty years, *Observations of an architect* examines iconic places, common experiences, and seemingly unrelated occurrences through an architectural lens, introducing broader thoughts on creative expression and on the practice of architecture.

For those who allow themselves to see the *extra*ordinary in the ordinary.

Observations

A Room Without Walls

I'm thinking back to when I was a boy on one of many family camping trips in the wilderness of Maine. It is late evening, and the sun has dipped behind the hills, leaving us to the glow of a warm campfire. Family and friends are circled around it, talking and laughing. My father stokes the fire with a long staff with a charred end, a gift from previous campers. I stare into the flames, mesmerized by their silent hypnotic dance. As I look around at everyone, I see faces and silhouettes caught in flickering light. We are in a place all our own, a room without walls. Its boundaries are set not by the light of the fire but by the reflection of light on ourselves. Just beyond our intimate room, a darkness surrounds us. What was ordinary ground only hours ago now seems like a mysterious, unknown world. In the distance are faint sounds of loons calling to each other. I feel the damp, chilly night air against my back and the warmth of the fire at my front. I'm completely content with those who share in the glow and conversation. There is nothing superficial about this moment. No advertisements, nothing to vie for our attention, no distractions. We created a special place where we could "be". It is one of my earliest experiences of presence.

We are born with great sensibilities to our environment. Each of us has the capacity to know presence.

The space beneath the canopy of a tree is a space like no other. It can be a refuge from a beating sun or a light rain. It can be a comfortable place to rest, with level ground and dappled sunlight, and just enough porosity to allow a gentle breeze to move through. Primitive yet delightful.

Tall, rust-colored trees shield everything but the open sky, directing my view down the monochrome passage. It calls me to enter this ephemeral atmosphere and cross its floor of scattered leaves. I accept with anticipation and become a silent traveler.

Lilli and I are walking toward Bethesda Terrace in Central Park. As we approach, the plaza opens up to our left, and we look down to see groups of people along the edge of The Lake and around Bethesda Fountain. Descending the grand steps to the plaza, we are greeted by the sound of a choir singing. Drawn by the music, we walk toward that beautiful passage beneath the terrace which connects the fountain plaza to the esplanade. Limestone arches and ornate blue ceiling tiles provide the perfect backdrop for the five singers harmonizing inside. Their voices resonate as if within a cathedral, amplifying out toward the plaza.

We find a seat along the edge of the fountain and become immersed in the sounds of conversation, the rhythm of drums, and the gentle cascade of falling water. This is the music of community.

Bethesda Terrace is a treasure to rediscover time and again. From nearly every approach, it remains hidden until you emerge from a winding path. This poetic setting blurs the boundaries between architecture, landscape, and engineering. Olmsted and Vaux would be proud to know that this place still serves as intended and continues to elevate the spirit.

Within the Interstitial

After a long drive, I am nearly at the beach. I gather my things and cross a paved parking lot towards the entrance of a long, narrow path through thick dune grasses. Tall and slender, they sway easily to the side as I navigate, and I can feel the cold dew on my legs as I brush against them. I place my steps methodically where others have stepped; my sandals sink slightly in sandy soil, still damp from early morning rain. I hear the cries of gulls nearby, and the slow, rhythmic pulse of the surf. Ahead of me, the meandering path reveals vivid green grasses below an open blue sky. My paced walk has put me into some trance, and my thoughts have drifted off. I am in no rush whatsoever to reach my destination.

Lying on the beach, the warm, salty breeze fills my senses completely. Powerful forces churn just beyond in the form of crashing waves and sea spray against large, smooth-faced boulders. A local fishing troller in the bay sits idle, its white body and long spider arms standing out against the blue-grey water. There is no reflection on the surface today. Driftwood lies scattered along the beach with the help of a morning high tide. In this moment, there is nowhere else I would rather be.

Resonance

She hovers gracefully across the stage in rhythmic spins, barely touching the floor. The delicate fabric of her costume trails behind her in slow motion like ripples of water flowing downstream. Her precise pace is perfectly in time with the tempo of the music. It seems so effortless for her. As the surrounding lights fade, she is left in the spotlight, and the deep, broad stage disappears around her. The stage is hers. She invites us into this intimate setting she created, and I am captivated.

Soon, other dancers flood the stage, and in an instant, the room is transformed. The solo performer weaves into the group as part of a larger rhythm. Each dancer holds their own space, yet it is the entire group I see. Their synchronized movement dazzles me in a unified expression, fluid and alive. As the lights brighten, illuminating the audience beyond the stage, my applause and quiet awe join the rest of the audience, changing the pulse of the room, and now the entire place resonates with energy.

Near the Tate Modern, I am struck by the incredible detailing and composition of the towers, but even more compelling is the sensibility of the pedestrian experience through the landscaped walks between the buildings. The rich variety of paths and gardens offers a true public realm where one can break from the confines of the city. Meandering through this made our walk that much more enjoyable.

At the Kimmel Center for the Performing Arts in Philadelphia, the large glazed barrel vault roof is reminiscent of the Musée d'Orsay in Paris. Inside the building, within the volume of the barrel-vault, are the two primary performance venues, the main symphony hall and the recital hall. Each venue is a sculptural object, and the space between them serves as pre-function space, lobby, and public plaza. I love the idea of an interstitial space serving multiple roles, and it feels like an extension of the street.

Knowing Beauty

My son is excited about an art class he is taking at our local museum. They are studying impressionism, and he started a watercolor of an ocean sunset based on a painting in the museum. He explains to me how the clouds should be orange, like the yolks of the eggs we have at home, and says he wants to change his painting so it is more like the sunset we saw at the beach. At seven years old, he is allowing his experiences to inform his work.

I ask him, "What's the difference between seeing a painting of an ocean sunset and watching a real sunset, standing barefoot on the sand?" He thinks for a moment, then says, "Looking at the painting is seeing something beautiful. Being there in person is knowing something beautiful." "What do you mean by *knowing* something is beautiful?" I ask. He says, "Well, when I'm on the beach, I can smell and hear the ocean, and it's real." "So they are both beautiful?" I ask. What about them tells you they are beautiful?" "I'm not sure," he says. "I just look at them and know they are beautiful. I don't need to think about it."

He is right, of course. When we encounter something or someone special, we know it instantly, even though we may not know why. My son also reminds me of the differences between imagery and experience. An image of a sunset only tells me a part of the story. It does not tell me how strangely alluring it is to witness the profound silence of the fading sun as it dips into the horizon, nor of the anticipation of counting down the seconds of its descent. Such moments are precious, but not rare. They happen all the time in small doses.

Beauty is recognized
without analysis.

Patina

I was fortunate during my childhood to have my grandparents nearby, and I saw them often. Most times when I visited, my grandmother was sitting in her rocking chair, almost directly across from the front door. It was understood throughout my family that the seat was designated for her only. I always considered it to be the family throne. It wasn't until many years later, after she passed away, that I sat in that chair. Just seeing it brought back memories of her rocking to a calming cadence as she knit, with the slightest squeak of the floor each time she rocked forward. I began to examine it as if for the first time, and was struck by something I had not noticed before. Over the many years of occupying that chair, she managed to wear off the finish at the ends of the armrests. I ran my hands over the worn wood and felt even closer to her.

I love to discover clues about the life of objects and places, and the people who use them. I have an appreciation for the scent of a building lobby, or for stone steps that are slightly concave from generations of footsteps. They are records of the overlooked, unintentional, everyday occurrences that have left their mark over time, creating unique places imbued with characteristics only they can have because of where they are. I've heard people label these things "charming" or as "having character" or "antique". I prefer to think of them as "patina". They are the protective coating that records our humanity.

Our lives are recorded through daily interaction with the places we occupy and the things we use.

The stone pavers of this street have been worn over time. They go unnoticed when walking on them because the surface still feels irregular, but when looking down the road, the smooth areas blend into a shiny surface like a still pond, and begin to reflect buildings beyond.

Part of what gives a place charm or character comes from how we use it. These unintended consequences reveal hints about the people who were here before us, and these details reinforce the authenticity and uniqueness of a place. I can only guess why these marks were made, but I know there is a story behind them, and that makes it all the more interesting.

From the street, I can't tell what purpose this building serves, or where the boundary lies between structure and setting. If not for the lit room, I might believe this is an abandoned relic being consumed by nature.

One morning, I find the Church of Saint Eustache nearly empty, giving me the opportunity to wander slowly through its cavernous Gothic volumes. There are many satisfying things to take in. I love how the morning light bathes the space through enormous stained-glass windows. I pause to notice the slight wearing of the floor before each seat, and lift my gaze again to soaring spaces. Stone, wood, glass, and light: like musical notes to be arranged in countless melodies.

Older roof tiles have been reused on a new structure underneath. The fresher, consistent color of the new creates a visual grid against the weathered tiles. The temporary contrast between old and new is enhanced by the irregular tonal qualities and shadows.

The Influence of Time

I am touring a high-rise residential building under construction in midtown Manhattan with a friend who is overseeing its development. As we pass through the lobby, he explains what is envisioned for the space. We ascend to an apartment in its raw, unfinished state and step outside to the balcony for a spectacular view of the city and Madison Park below. Taller towers reflect the orange of a low-lying sun, peaking above an undulating flow of smaller buildings. I look directly across at a tall building capped with a clock tower. I doubt whoever designed and built it anticipated that one day people would be so close to this clock tower. And yet the details that could have been dismissed, ones that might not be noticed in a hundred years, are all there. If only every building could be constructed with such integrity.

At dusk, the angled path of Broadway has become a dark ravine, cutting through the grid of mid-rise buildings, which deny the streets of the last remaining daylight. The Indigenous People who first occupied this land could never have imagined a building like this. Nor could those early settlers of New Amsterdam, who would have considered this location well beyond their protected walls. And now here I am high in the sky on a thin slab of concrete. Only months ago, this floor did not exist. I was in new territory. In the history of the world, I was in a location that no other person had ever stood, and where few will ever occupy. The idea still gives me chills. And yet this high-rise is one of many in the city, slowly influencing others around it. Like Broadway itself, whose structures have transitioned from wood to brick, brick to stone, stone to steel, and steel to glass, it proves that change and innovation happen incrementally, and acceptance of that change is relative. In the words of Ralph Waldo Emerson, "If the stars should appear but one night every thousand years, how man would marvel and stare."

Innovation is incremental
and embracing change is
relative to context.

The grandfather of the modern skyscraper, the Seagram Building by Mies van der Rohe, remains bold and majestic. Although the materials and assemblies used to build it will eventually become obsolete, the ideas that brought it into existence live on in generations of other buildings.

A boy runs freely in the wide courtyard, likely unaware that below him are ruins of a moat and fortress dating back to the 12th Century.

Across the street from my desk at Rafael Viñoly Architects' office on Vandam Street in New York, I would see the renovation of a former warehouse building constructed in 1910. It sits on the site of one of the original plantations of the New Amsterdam Colony, though that history would be difficult to discern if not for a plaque near the rear of the building. Built for its time, the enduring nature of its solid brick walls and grid-like structure has made it easily adaptable and helped to ensure its longevity. With some precise modifications, as indicated by the saw at the facade, this building will be transformed for a different purpose and live to see another day.

This is a structure I thought I knew well, and when I saw it from a distance, I naively presumed to know what to expect. I underestimated the grandeur of its base and the intricate details of the cast-iron elements. I wasn't prepared for how beautifully it would transform from late afternoon to evening.

Elegant in its composition of form and structure, the Eiffel Tower expanded the boundaries of engineering and construction in the 1880s. It was the tallest man-made structure in the world at that time, built with prefabricated elements made in Eiffel's workshop. However, the proposal for the tower was not all well-received. Its ambitious height and aesthetic expression drew opposition from influential people such as novelist Alexandre Dumas and Charles Garnier, architect of the Paris Opera House.

Although hugely popular with the general public, the tower was originally intended to be dismantled after twenty years as part of the 1889 World Exhibition. Gustav Eiffel had to prove the tower's long-term value to the Parisian government to secure its continued existence, which involved successfully conducting scientific experiments, meteorological observations, and a telegraph station.

Today, the Eiffel Tower symbolizes the power architecture has to influence, and eventually, represent a culture.

Developed through HH Richardson's personal interpretation of Romanesque in a style later known as Richardsonian, Trinity Church is considered by many to be one of the most influential buildings in American architecture. Years later, the Hancock Tower would push the limits of minimalist expression with large glass units and a tall, slender form, becoming Boston's tallest building. Due to the strong resistance to the proximity of the tower to the church, Henry Cobb revised the tower design to limit shadows on the church. To see Richardson's masterwork reflected in the glassy facade seems a continued homage to past efforts of individual expression.

An exterior stair at Carnegie Hall in New York City is a remnant of older building codes and remains in use today. Its length and gracefulness embody a unique element on an otherwise blank facade. Still, I cannot imagine rushing out of a burning building to find myself so high above the street on such a delicate and narrow stair.

Originally established as one of Europe's first hospitals for orphans and the poor, Santa Maria Della Scala now exists as a museum. Strangely, its long history of serving others before self is not lost in this image. The hospital's original facade and windows now seem in dire need of care. Yet the plain rectangular glazing, surrounded by dingy brick infill, reflects the brilliant entrance of Siena Cathedral and the roots of the hospital.

Some places have the markings of a certain genre, or style, or period, and yet are universally relatable and appreciated by many people. They have certain qualities that make them remarkable. These two beloved museum spaces share a similar purpose and are practically neighbors, yet they are worlds apart in terms of architectural expression.

Even though the older lockset no longer functions properly, I appreciate the gesture of leaving it in place. The juxtaposition between the old and new speaks to me about a shift in cultural attitudes. Like many products today, the newer version is slimmer, smaller, and nicely packaged. There is little interest in showing how it works; there is only an expectation for performance. The old lock shows the spring and bolt, and a hint of how it might work. It shows how robust it is as a deterrent, suggesting that its larger size may provide better security.

Seduction of the Authentic

We gather as a group around a large model of the ancient complex. I listen as our guide notes the importance of Copan as a major Mayan city and of its significant contribution to our understanding of astronomy and mathematics. She describes a monumental hieroglyphic stair with the longest inscription in the Mayan region. Throughout the city ruins are intricate carvings, still stained with once-vibrant colors that exemplify the inevitable decay of previous glory. Even after centuries of erosion, this complex shows the best of human ambition and enterprise, as well as the expansive capacities of the human spirit. The weathered walls portray the ebb and flow of a civilization and its culture.

I have an underlying awareness when walking on sacred soil, a reverence for the past that grounds me in the present. I feel this place wants me to fill it with imagined scenarios of how life might have been, and I slip into another world. Images come to mind of an expansive settlement, alive with bustling markets and livestock, children playing, and the movement of people in their daily routines. Ordinary life has never been so extraordinary.

Places we connect with remind
us of our own humanity.

A morning view of Phillips Exeter Academy Library. The teak paneling shows evidence of heavy rainfall moments earlier. Most images of this building showcase the incredible atrium inside, but the exterior is just as compelling to me. I understand its strength and permanence by the thickness of the brick walls and shortened openings along its base. I sense its heaviness in the shadows of its deep recesses. It feels like a modern ruin.

The washing of natural light on wood is an open invitation by the window to approach it, to stand beside it, and see what else it has to offer.

Signatures

There is a woman in my office who has somehow memorized people's footsteps when they walk along the corridor towards her desk. She can tell who they are without even lifting her head to see them. Some have a heavy, lumbering pace. Others have a sharp, loud cadence. She didn't memorize them intentionally. She simply recognized patterns over time and made the associations. Their walks are signatures, announcing their individuality. How many times have each of us noticed something similar? We might know a particular step that creaks in our house or the scent of a room. These subtleties guide us to what is authentic.

Good places are loyal to us. They are there for us daily, sharing in our experiences. We learn to trust them after we've had time to pass by, stop in, and get to know them. Even after we part ways, there are certain things about the places we encounter that stay with us, even if those things mean little at the time. I can still recall in my mind the scent of floor wax used on the corridors of my elementary school. A sort of floral fragrance with a hint of commercial grade chemicals. Not a great first impression, I would say, but impressionable just the same. I'm not sure why I still know that scent. The main entrance, I'm sure, still permeates with it, or at least I hope so. It is one of those strange things that I have come to know that identifies that place for me in my memories.

The beckoning light of the opening beyond is made more apparent by the diagonal edge of the shadow on the wall. The darkened area to the right is curiously similar to the shape of the adjacent opening, as though it were a negative imprint.

How many generations of footsteps have passed these steps to soften the edges of the treads so nicely?

A History in Things

I know of an immense stone quarry in the Green Mountains of Vermont. At nearly six hundred feet deep, its white, faceted walls are like giant chisel marks, stained with ink running down its grooved faces. Large derricks cast their wired web over the open void. The entire scene could almost be mistaken for a construction site, as though they are piecing the hillside back together.

There is another quarry I know, smaller and abandoned. Nature began to reclaim it long ago. Its sloped walls, now softened by vegetation, remind me of the ruins of a lost civilization. Tree growth along the top blurs the once bold edge, and dark water has somehow found a home within this carved basin. Perhaps the earth is trying to heal itself. There is a mist that sits just above the water, and echoes resonate with the sounds of a tossed stone. It takes on an eerie tone, yet it is still and peaceful. Each time I walk along the footpath to the clearing, I discover it all over again, and it is nothing less than magical.

Stone from these quarries has crossed many borders. They have become polished monuments and kitchen counters, courthouse steps and lobby walls. Whenever I see something made of stone, in its finished form, I often think about where its origin may be. By satisfying our need to define our existence in this world, we also leave our mark through the void that remains. Our primitive urge to dig is necessary for the structures we create and for the extraction of materials used to build them. And yet these quarries, at least the abandoned ones, seem almost a natural setting, as though they are meant to exist. I am often reminded that natural resources are precious and that materials have a history of their own.

What we leave behind is a
reflection of ourselves.

A post, cut and dried, sawn, punctured, clamped, stained, nailed, and worn - still standing, still useful, still beautiful

The opening in this ancient city wall was originally meant for surveillance of attacking vessels. It has now become a lens through which to view blue.

A Way of Seeing

I love the feeling of a well-fitted handrail as I ascend a stair, or the texture of the wood grain in a well-made piece of furniture. To run my hand across it tells me more than I can know by simply looking. I sense its density, the temperature of its surface, and the quality of its connections. I know that someone cared about how it was made, and understanding this makes all the difference. If I believe someone cares about what they create, I may also think that person cares about how I experience their creation, and that, ultimately, they care about me.

I rely on touch to help me understand, and probably more so now than when I was younger. Every object has embedded information, a story to tell, and I feel as though I need to make physical contact to extract its secrets. This information I cannot seem to acquire by any other means, and it is partly how I come to know beauty.

Dignity

Our group arrived at a small village just outside of San Pedro Sula in Honduras. Over the next week or so, we will renovate an existing one-room building into a primary school, complete with playground equipment, desks, books, and enough funding for an entire year. Each morning, the neighborhood children would greet us and interact throughout the day. One girl, Maria, was a soft-spoken leader among the other children. She had a special charm and determination that made her shine, and she managed to rally other children to join us in the renovation effort.

Reaching the schoolhouse required walking through a dense network of one-story shacks that lined narrow dirt streets. Deep ditches ran on either side of the street to guide heavy rainwater into a channel leading to a nearby river. There was one particular home I passed by each day that caught my attention. It was a two-room shack with a corrugated aluminum roof. A small opening in the corner allowed smoke to rise out. The walls were made of tree branches, tied together with a sort of burlap rope. These were clad with large rough-sawn boards. Each room was roughly three meters by three meters, with a slightly raised dirt floor. It was not unlike the construction of other shacks; in fact, some were in better condition and had actual walls and concrete floors. What caught my eye was how impeccably clean it was. From the street was a manicured entrance area, clearly defined and smooth. Bicycles had an allocated place. At the doorway was a woven thatched rug with some shoes aligned against the wall.

The woman who lived here had done well with what she had to make it feel like "home". On our last day visiting, this woman met us along the street. With a smile, she spoke with our local guide to express her thanks to us. She mentioned how happy she was that her children would be able to go to school, especially her daughter Maria, who wants to travel and be a teacher.

Years later, in New York, I am walking through a public housing complex on my way to the office. The narrow street of cracked asphalt is flanked by identical six-story brick blocks. The windows are tiny. The entrances are narrow. Chain-link fences surround each building, enclosing barren strips of open soil and a few awkwardly placed shrubs. Thoughts of Maria and her mother enter my mind, and the word dignity. How did the people who contributed to the making of this place manage to create something so inadequate? How can this be? Where is the space for the human spirit to thrive? Where is the consideration and care for the individual?

From the Latin word **dignitas** is the meaning **worthiness**. Such a beautiful word to initiate the creation of a building. How can a building be designed to acknowledge the dignity in each of us? Perhaps the secret lies in a welcoming entry, well-maintained areas, and an elevated floor. Maybe it requires a sense of ownership, or a connection with nature. I believe it starts with listening to the inner voice telling me this is a place I want to be.

I am always amazed at the rich palette of colors and textures stone offers. The image of the stone slab above conjures impressions of an old, twisted tree. The image on the opposite page seems like ripples on a pond, or a lost color field painting. The selection of materials and how they will be used is something to consider seriously since they must ultimately come together as a composition.

Incidental Connections

I wait for a few other people to step away before I approach the massive red painting by Barnett Newman entitled *Vir Heroicus Sublimis*. I step close enough to it so that the ends disappear as I look forward. I am engulfed by bold red. Almost immediately, I feel its overbearing presence. Strangely, my breathing changes. I start to become overwhelmed, and I'm compelled to turn to the side and step away. Lilli says I looked dazed and asks if I am feeling okay. I've never had such a reaction to a painting before, and it certainly affected me.

I believe in the power of quiet observation. My curiosity often leads me to unusual observations about people and their behaviors, and about culture and nature, which I can bring into my work as an architect.

Architecture relies on its physicality to express intangible qualities that define its relevance and beauty. That same beauty can be found in the everyday, in secondary structures, in open space, in objects, and in art. Although I relate to places through my physical engagement with them, my relationship with architecture begins with objects that are not buildings but affect me directly, and is cultivated by a curiosity about what they are and why they influence me.

How we experience is as important
as what we experience.

From this angle, the mirrored dresser achieves a higher level of transparency with the alignment of the floor edge. The apparent corner of the room reflected in the dresser face is nearly in the same location as the actual corner just beyond the dresser.

Neatly arranged rows of aluminum chairs fill a plaza. The softly curved form is brushed by sunlight and features a slight gradation that becomes darker along the top edge. The whole arrangement is pristine and ordered. Soon, it will be flooded with multitudes of fabrics and colors as people unknowingly disrupt the beautiful collection.

Even the most benign common spaces can take on a certain charm and can be beautiful. This open platform of ordinary steel grating is a simple, delicate structure. It is that way to make it affordable, using only what is necessary. And yet it takes on a certain beauty in its own right due to its purity and humble function.

A view of **Storm King Wall** at Storm King Art Center. I appreciate
how Andy Goldsworthy approaches his art by using elemental,
primitive materials to create something bold, geometric, natural,
and authentic.

Installation view at Storm King Art Center, Mountainville, NY
© Andy Goldsworthy, Courtesy Galerie Lelong

Authorlessness

If I am lucky, I may be able to design perhaps fifty or sixty buildings during my lifetime. And if they are to have a lasting influence, they should be built for longevity and be flexible in use. I think of them as instruments for the movement of people, sound, and light. In these places will be a small offering of myself, each infused with my particular set of ideas. Yet people will interact with them without knowing me as a person. Just as a musician doesn't own the sounds created through an instrument, I do not own how the light embraces a building and spills into its rooms. I do not own the harmonious sounds of people gathered in a plaza, or the refreshing breeze sweeping through a courtyard on a warm summer day. So long as people appreciate these types of things in places I create, they need not know me at all. My task is to compose and let Mother Nature play it through as she does best.

As I step into the balcony corridor from my Chicago hotel room, I am confronted by this lobby atrium, offering a sample of the activities below. The instant transition from a conventional hotel room to this massive void is unsettling to me, even after several days here. The scale of it is so large that it feels like I am peering into a living dollhouse, complete with model furniture and figurines at the bar.

A bland building with its rudimentary fire escape is transformed by the midday sun. The intense sunlight and wiry elements of the stair bear crisp shadows against the light-colored facade, and at first glance, it appears as though the stair and its shadows are one. The result is a distortion of what is real and what is projected.

Looking down over the patchwork of farmlands near this small town in Germany, I see no official borders or labels, only an expansive landscape. From above, I can appreciate the weaving of roads influenced by the farms, and how the town fits within a larger network of communities. From my temporary vantage point, this place reminds me of small New England farming towns and feels more familiar than foreign.

Houses in Bermuda are built with stepped limestone roofs. The weight helps against forceful winds, and the stepped nature allows the collection of precious rainwater. While learning about this from a local guide, I happened to be taking this picture, admiring the composition of blues and greens. Only later did I realize the brilliance of how the tree fans out to nearly every opening to catch water, yet the branches are flexible to sway in heavy winds.

Compositions of tree bark. Each tree in the immediate area has unique color patterns from light to dark, but together they appear uniform.

More than a dozen rowboats randomly scattered along the edge of a pond began to align themselves with the shifting of the wind. In the course of fifteen minutes, the vessels bumped and creaked into order like soldiers in slow motion.

Acquaintances

For years, it stood at the shoulder of the road, and as time went on, I could see its posture deteriorate while fields and overgrowth surrounded it. Its creaky timber frame eventually leaned so far over that it seemed impossible it was able to stand at all. The barn was once part of a large farm that has long since vanished. For anyone traveling Route 11, it was hard to miss, partly because of its close proximity to the road.

I've wondered about the farmer who owned it when it was in prime condition. Did he have the same fate as this simple barn, hunched over from years of neglect? Sometimes, as I passed by the barn, I felt as though I were visiting the old farmer to check in on him and see how he was doing. During a recent trip along this road, my wife asked me if we had passed the barn yet, and I realized I had not seen it on our way through. It was only on our return that I saw the pile of board siding and stone foundation that remained. Someone had likely taken it down since it was so dilapidated. Lilli said it was good that someone had prevented it from collapsing into the road, and she was right. But as I agreed with her, an unexpected sadness washed over me. I will miss this barn.

The Act of Discovering

I walk along a country road on a beautiful June afternoon. Loose pebbles under my feet alert me to my pace with a subtle crunching sound. Slight breezes pass over grassy shoulders, carrying the sweet smell of freshly cut hay from the nearby field. Large elms run rhythmically along the sides of the road, reaching up with outstretched branches to weave a delicate canopy completely cloaking the road. I am in a natural colonnade. Speckles of sunlight break through the leaves, disappearing and reappearing with a gentle sway of branches.

Autumn brings cooler temperatures. Foliage is on full display in bold golds, deep coppers, and crimsons. In only a few weeks, the leaves will fade to duller tones, lose their strength, and be cast off with the wind. I walk towards the crest of a hill where the road opens to an expansive view of undulating hills, seemingly transformed overnight from vibrant greens to gentle waves of softened hues. I stand there for a moment quietly in admiration, with the autumn air on my face and that unmistakable scent of damp leaves scattered on the ground.

Winter along the road reveals a completely different place. Colorful canopies have disappeared, and sunlight spills in through tangled branches. Grassy shoulders rise high in the form of steep snow banks. The road is like an empty white riverbed, scabbed over in a thick layer of compacted snow, revealing tracks of previous travelers. I sense the give of the treads against the snow through my fingertips on the steering wheel, and cherish the sound of silent tires coasting.

In the daily pace of my life, some places afford me a different way to measure time. Even a path between places can offer such moments. I must patiently wait another year to have these experiences again, and, of course, I am happy to do so.

A good place invites nature to influence it and transform it into something remarkable.

At a family restaurant in Kopito, Montenegro, we ate under an unadorned pavilion. This is a view from our seat of a barn beyond. I was struck by the composition of geometric shapes. The various planes of facade and shadow have an apparent flatness to them, and it reminds me of a collage of sorts. Simple shapes in light strike a balance with the textural effects of the grasses and wood tables.

These variations of stone for three uses create a harmonious composition from wall to terrace to path. The rough parging of the wall, the bogen patterning of smooth round rocks, and the square flat pavers come together to form a strata. The raised pieces in the path are necessary to divert heavy rains and balance the horizontal divisions of the curbing and wall cap.

A new building is being constructed near my home. Designed by a highly influential architect, the development will be rental housing, and one can already get a sense of the building from the integration of the structure and facade. The repetitive nature of the building speaks to a rational, methodical approach, but the overall form suggests intentions to be dynamic and unusual.

The light reflects brilliantly on the multi-marbled facade of the Basilica of Santa Croce in Florence, Italy. Accessing the piazza through narrow streets frames views like this and accentuates one's focus on what lies ahead.

The reflection of the building across the street adds intrigue to this image, but it is the elegant detailing that captures my interest. The frame of this entrance door serves as an anchor for the cable structure for the glass facade. The unconventional detail is thoughtful, providing only what is essential. Developing such a detail goes beyond normal obligations. Extraordinary buildings require extraordinary effort.

Simple. Poetic. The colors of stained glass strike a plain stone wall at Notre Dame Cathedral.

Landscape view along the Grand Canal at Versailles. The landscape can be viewed as a two-dimensional abstract mass of grass, water, trees, and sky. Distant landscapes are usually seen in this reduced manner, leaving only what is necessary and what the eye can absorb.

Nature is full of examples of balanced compositions that are nearly symmetrical, yet irregular. This image of the lake in my hometown embodies a Japanese principle called "Fukinsei", a basic tenet of traditional Japanese Zen aesthetic that celebrates beauty through balanced asymmetry.

From street level, the Oculus at the World Trade Center Transportation Hub is mostly hidden, presenting an element of surprise when entering. The geometric purity of its form and the abundance of natural light evoke an almost spiritual presence for me. Each time I pass through this underground public square, I feel uplifted.

Collective Gestures

I have a great appreciation for composers, particularly composers for film. They bring their own sensibilities to a score while also supporting the story of the film. Along with the producer, the composer must also collaborate with the musicians performing the pieces. They are experts in their own right, bringing something unique to the piece and adding subtle detail to the composition. And yet when I hear the music, I'm not thinking of any of this. I'm taken back instantly to a different time and place. With only a few broad strokes of deep cello, a harmonized violin quartet, and solo violin, my attention turns inward. Music is my insistent friend.

I have a different relationship with Architecture. It relies on repeated encounters around and in, and through. I know these buildings well, and yet there is always something else to notice. It may be a particular sequence of spaces, a singular room, or a unique detail. My attention turns inward. Architecture is my unassuming friend.

Within architectural compositions are moments of beauty, individual elements that are both unique and expressive. They are akin to the sound of a fine violin or a deep cello: resonant, emotional, and distinct. These moments arise from the contributions of many craftspeople and artists, each bringing something singular to the creation of a building and enriching its overall expression. Such collective gestures imbue a place with a complexity that cannot be fully captured in images or understood through a single encounter.

A work of Architecture is made by
many people so that it may be
experienced through one person.

This large wooden door contains a small passage door to use when it is closed. Only the slightest gap can be seen at the edge. Although a common detail for this type of building, it responds to a specific need and blends in, not detracting from the overall composition.

A main ingredient for good design is caring about what is left behind. There are many more interesting things to design than a roadway swale, yet this one I found worthy of a photograph. I like the consistency of the material and the proportions of the stone pavers for the street, the swale, and the curb. I appreciate the small slotted drains, designed for minimal visual impact yet spaced adequately to function properly.

The thick brick walls, heavy stone sill, and large, plain metal door all have a wonderful pairing, which speaks to the industrial use of the building. It makes sense when one sees it. What makes this stand out for me is how the rounded brick corner and the arched opening, as the shadow reveals, play off the malleable metal door. Both have a softness which is unexpected for a strong, heavy mill building.

A skylight well is designed to cultivate a refreshing and welcoming atmosphere below. Set against a gold-colored ceiling, the offset apertures invite light to wash the smooth conical surfaces, expressing varying intensities of light and shadow. The delicate edge at the junction of the openings is particularly intriguing.

Fredrick Law Olmsted believed that one needed to "aim for the unconscious" when designing landscapes. He believed the simple things we tend to overlook and take for granted have a profound influence on us. I love this notion of appealing to the unconscious. These images capture three different elements within a building provided by separate craftsmen. They contribute to this unconscious appeal through the repetition of form and patterns in seating, flooring, and ceiling, strengthening the experience as a whole.

While visiting a Basilica in Cartago, Costa Rica, my attention was naturally diverted to the ceiling and open volume of space. It was only after some time that I noticed that every seat, back, back cap, and kneeler of the pews were made of single boards. The thought that such a subtle detail could be easily missed makes it all the more wonderful to me.

Rather than being subjected to products or advertisements, this glowing column of light awaits at the top of a stair as one ascends to the mezzanine in a clothing store. The color temperature of the light is intentionally similar to daylight. It is meant to re-energize and give pause during the shopping experience. As an additional way to relate on a subconscious level, the aperture is roughly the same width as a person.

Shadows are at play between exhibit stands at a museum. Made for utility with an intent to blend in, these plain, ordinary stands have a beauty that presents itself under the right conditions. Focused lighting for the exhibits is softened against the flat white planes and crisp edges. Whomever placed them in the room was so careful to space them evenly and make sure they were well organized.

A Way of Doing

My father worked most of his adult life in a sawmill. He was responsible for maintaining the quality and precision of massive saws capable of devouring entire logs in minutes to produce lumber. He taught me about the beauty and strength of wood, introducing me to the quarter-sawn and rift-sawn woods, as well as mortise-and-tenon and dovetail joinery. One of my favorite joinery techniques is what he called a "Hell joint", because once set, it cannot be dismantled without destroying it. As a concealed joint, it must be set properly on the first try.

There is a furniture maker in New York City, Miya Shoji, who has mastered this joinery technique. The family of highly skilled Japanese craftsmen maintains an authentic, traditional approach to woodworking. Using only the finest naturally dried wood and hand tools, they rely on their knowledge of the materials to create exquisitely crafted products. Without nails, machines, or power tools, each piece is made with only wood. There is a reverence for wasting as little as possible, and for reflecting a natural order in what is produced. A table, for example, is made from a single tree, and the base of the table is from the base of the tree. The table not only forms seamlessly, but the legs snap into place using a single, thin wood band held in tension. They understand the capabilities of wood so well that they can express the essential nature of it.

As an architect, I define spaces that rely on the fundamental understanding of many materials. I provide detailed drawings and assemblies for construction and rely on the craftsmanship of others who contribute their expertise. Through an understanding of light and shadow, the intersection of volumes, and the movement of the body, I hope to express those intangible qualities that speak to the human spirit. It is a process of uncertainty, trust, close collaboration, and continued optimism.

Design is the filter through
which complexity is expressed
in clear and simple ways.

Today, we consider scaffolding as being rough and uninteresting, and therefore not having much value in our built environment. This temporary framework surrounding the Colonne Vendôme in Paris is designed to hide an elevator and provide a shroud of gridded scaffolding. It strikes me as being quite elegant and continues the role of "monument".

The older portion of Mostar, Bosnia and Herzegovina, is a UNESCO World Heritage site. Many buildings, such as this mill building, have been renovated using a traditional method for roofing by using thick local stone slabs on a wood purlin framework. The result is a beautifully harmonious monolithic assembly of small stone buildings that present themselves as a natural outcropping of the banks of the Neretva River.

These are test samples of different cleaning methods for the facade of a large iconic building. The variations are striking, even though it is the same stone, and whatever method is selected can have a dramatic impact on how the building is received. Even something that seems relatively simple, such as cleaning a facade, requires an investment of time and patience to do it well and to achieve the desired effect.

I am always impressed by the technical knowledge required to produce well-designed things. Without proper technical investigation, even a thoughtful design can fall short during construction. Without solid design principles, technical considerations can become mired in indecision, lose their purpose, and result in mediocrity. I believe good design finds a balance of the technical and the idea; the how and the why. One keeps it grounded in reality so it can be made, while the other pushes boundaries to ensure the end result transcends normality.

During the 19th century, the Amoskeag Manufacturing Company was the largest cotton textile mill in the world. It's very establishment spurred the founding of Manchester, New Hampshire, the state's largest city. Company engineers methodically designed and constructed dozens of buildings over time using a common local red brick to unify the complex. Many buildings have been successfully converted for other uses, including an architecture firm where I once worked. Built for efficiency in the interest of production, these straightforward structures, such as this slightly tapering circular brick stack, still manage to impress.

A simple palette of materials can provide clarity of the spatial qualities of a room or space. Seemingly carved from some monolithic stone, this entrance corridor at Versailles achieves elegance and sophistication with minimal detail and straightforward use of repetition and volumes.

Inspired by artist Donald Judd, the glass shelves cantilever directly from the wall with no apparent method of connection. The retail display seems almost incidental, playing a secondary role to the horizontality of the glass planes.

Buildings include increasingly complex systems as technologies advance, and become challenging at times to organize them in complementary ways. This image of an exposed ceiling exemplifies how intricate the organization of such systems is evolving. The composition of piping and structure has become an exercise of design in its own right.

When the palette is simplified and the vocabulary is easy to understand, the ornate detailing stands out and becomes special. One is allowed to absorb the detail. When I see the repair in the cornice, I know that someone cares. Having someone recognize that I cared in my work is one of the most important things I can communicate as an architect.

The duality of the repetitious coffered ceiling as both a structural element and light well is something that appeals to me. Resolving multiple design issues through a singular poetic solution takes patience and persistence to get the details right. Seen from different angles, the ceiling seems to change dramatically, setting a uniform tone to the reception area below.

This stair exaggerates the experience of being in transition by evoking a cavernous feeling. Through the use of various scales of terrazzo cladding and low-level lighting along the treads, the stair takes on a sculptural quality that one must meander through. The warmth of the coated handrail adds a human touch.

The deep recess of the entrance serves a dual purpose. Setting the entrance back provides protection and creates a secondary space, while enhancing the monumentality of the brick. It offers both security and permanence, appropriate for this courthouse.

On Storytelling

I am working on the design for a housing project, a renovation of a beautiful brick building in Brooklyn, erected in the mid-1800s. Originally constructed as a religious college, it has also served as a private boarding school, a home for a non-profit organization, and a thrift store. It has now lain empty and abandoned for several years.

I visit the site to become familiar with the building and neighborhood. I am so pleasantly surprised! This building was once the matriarch of the neighborhood, with an elegance that clearly distinguishes it from surrounding structures. The facades are richly detailed with warm brick. The slate roof still carries its sheen, complementing the walls. I make my way up the stone entrance steps, chipped and cracked from neglect, and pass through the front door. Inside, the halls are wide, with heavy wooden doors, layered casings, and ornate cove ceilings. At the center lies a spacious private courtyard hidden from public view. This building has class!

Walking through its rooms, the conditions are dismal. The wood floors are buckled, and there is considerable damage from rainwater that has seeped through two floors from several holes in the roof. Although its spirit remains strong, the body is beginning to falter. I return several times to investigate its history, how it was made, and its condition in detail.

Imagination, curiosity and **empathy**.
These are my essential tools.
Imagination dreams of what may be.
Curiosity asks how it can be.
Empathy guides why it should be.

I wonder, "What stories do you have to tell?" Each time, I am filled with ideas for its renewed life, and I imagine new spaces within the existing walls.

I will spend the better part of a year proposing solutions, refining ideas, revising, and collaborating with others to offer new life to this building. It is an honor to be entrusted with continuing the story of a building, or a neighborhood, or a city, through a creative process. Anyone who has ever been fortunate enough to realize a creative endeavor, to see it materialize as an offering for others, knows how deeply satisfying it is to revisit the work later in life. There is so much we put of ourselves into the work we find fulfilling. When I complete a project, a part of me goes with it, and I am often left with an emptiness as I try to reconcile the emotional investment. Melancholy mixed with pride.

Any worthwhile endeavor requires personal investment to achieve something meaningful. The very word "invest" has a Latin root meaning "to clothe in" or "to wear". I like this definition as it relates to my work. It implies an empathic response as a means to uncover the right solution. I must remain open to suggestions and criticism if I am to become aware of how I might affect others through my work, a notion both unsettling and empowering. Empathy is key to finding meaning.

Richness can be found within the context of a site; deeply rooted knowledge right within reach that can inform the design of a place. Such knowledge offers a glimpse of what it means to be "somewhere," a term that is becoming increasingly difficult to define. As an architect, I must somehow forecast what a building or space will be like in the future. I have no choice but to rely on what exists now, and so I begin with questions before I can provide answers. Where is the land it will sit upon? What other structures will surround it? There are less tangible aspects to take note of, the culture of the people in the area, the attitudes and expectations of a client, and so on. I rely on this information as a basis for my own understanding of how a place might be. I imagine this new building embodying elegance and living a dignified life, and perhaps offering this same elegance and dignity to those people who walk through its doors and cross its grounds. I like to believe this is possible.

The practice of architecture is a continuation of the stories of our culture, and we change them with every place we create. What I make now may become something else later. It may be destroyed. It may be preserved or take on additions. It may become a neglected, worn-down building in Brooklyn. If I have done my work correctly, seeking to understand what makes a particular place special, then I will have succeeded in telling my part of the story of a place. I only hope that when my work does eventually see its transition, the people who oversee it can listen to the tales it has to tell.

A special thank you to my family, Lilli, William and Charlie, and to the following people who have contributed insight and support:

Barry Brensinger	Stephen Skolas
Scott Frances	Gabriel Smith
Matthew Gagnon	Billie Tsien
Frank Lupo	Tod Williams
Thomas Phifer	Andrew Zuckerman

Maurice Gagnon is an American architect based in New England. He founded Gagnon Architecture with a belief that people deserve authentic and inspiring places. Known for its collaborative approach, the firm specializes in creating unique places that are relatable, efficient, and expressive.

With more than twenty-five years of experience designing national and international projects, Maurice brings a depth of knowledge to high-performance cultural and arts-related projects. His work has been recognized by the American Institute of Architects, the Council on Tall Buildings and Urban Habitat, and the U.S. Green Building Council. A frequent lecturer and visiting juror at numerous universities, Maurice is an active member of the American Institute of Architects, the American Alliance of Museums, and the Architectural League of New York. He is a registered architect in multiple states and continues to advocate for design that elevates the human experience.